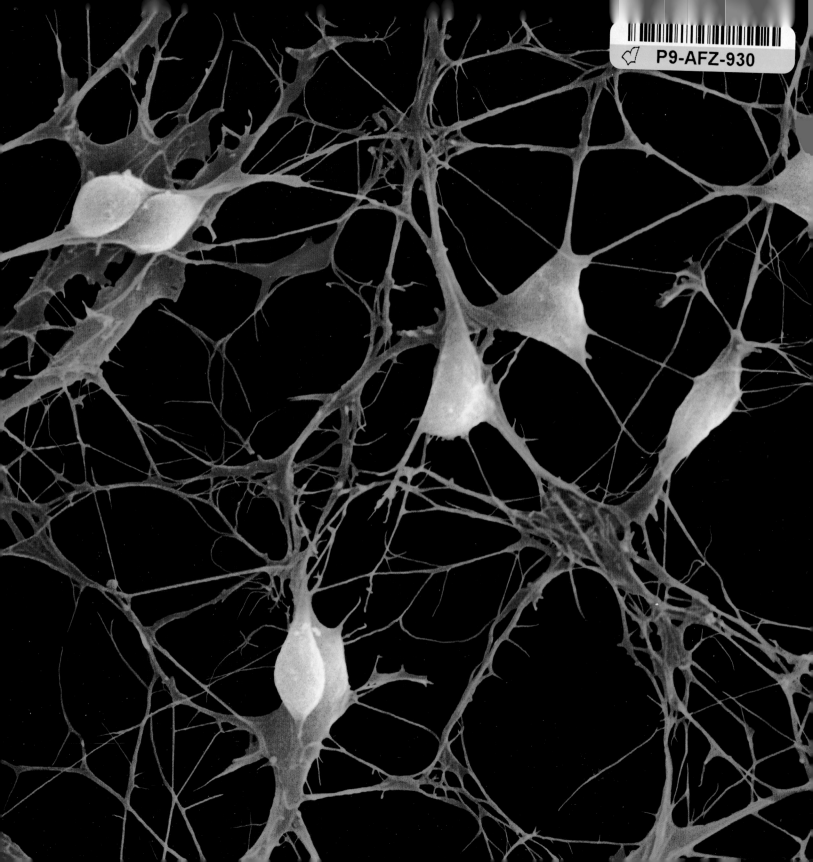

The symbol x shown
on each micrograph
indicates magnification.
"x1,770" means that the
object in the picture is
1,770 times its actual
size. All the micrographs
in this book have been
colorized for effect.
x1,770

SNEEZE!

Alexandra Siy
and Dennis Kunkel

ɪ▱ɪ Charlesbridge

To Eric—A. S.

To my grandnephew, Ian, and grandniece, Ellie—D. K.

Acknowledgments
A macroscopic thank-you to our splendid editor, Yolanda LeRoy, and art director, Susan Sherman: you're certainly nothing to sneeze at! Thanks also to neuroscience expert Eric H. Chudler, PhD, for his review of the book.

Alex is very grateful to all the beautiful and talented children whom she photographed for this book, whether they appear on these pages or not, and to their parents. Special thanks to Tracie Killar, director of the New Day Art after-school program in Albany, NY; Mary Bayham-Caraco, fellow biologist and mother of six; Danielle Schwartzbauer, fellow Winterberry Charter School parent and mother of four; Hope Konecny, dedicated mom and fencing coach; and Alex's dear friend, 90-year-old Marian Vaughn, who has leopard frogs living in her basement.

Dennis thanks Chris Porter of Chris Porter Illustration for colorizations of the electron micrographs. Special thanks to Dennis's wife, Nancy Eckmann, who provided valuable insight in her review of this book.

Published by Charlesbridge
85 Main Street
Watertown, MA 02472
(617) 926-0329
www.charlesbridge.com

Library of Congress Cataloging-in-Publication Data
Siy, Alexandra.
    Sneeze / Alexandra Siy and Dennis Kunkel.
        p. cm.
    ISBN: 978-1-57091-653-3 (reinforced for library use)
    ISBN: 978-1-57091-654-0 (softcover)
1. Sneezing—Juvenile literature. I. Kunkel, Dennis.
II. Title.
QP123.8.S59 2006
612.2—dc22   2005027567

Printed in China
(hc) 10 9 8 7 6 5 4 3 2 1
(sc) 10 9 8 7 6 5 4 3 2 1

Type set in Sabon and Humana
Printed and bound by Jade Productions
Production supervision by Brian G. Walker
Designed by Susan Mallory Sherman

Lily closes her eyes—WAIT! What's that inside Lily's nose?

It's pollen, and it's causing her to have an allergic reaction—her immune system's exaggerated response to a usually harmless substance. Although Lily's body is behaving as if it's being invaded by disease-causing germs, it isn't. Pollen does not cause infection. Pollen grains are powdery particles produced by flowering plants for reproduction. In allergic people, pollen triggers the lining inside the nose to release histamine, the chemical that causes congestion.

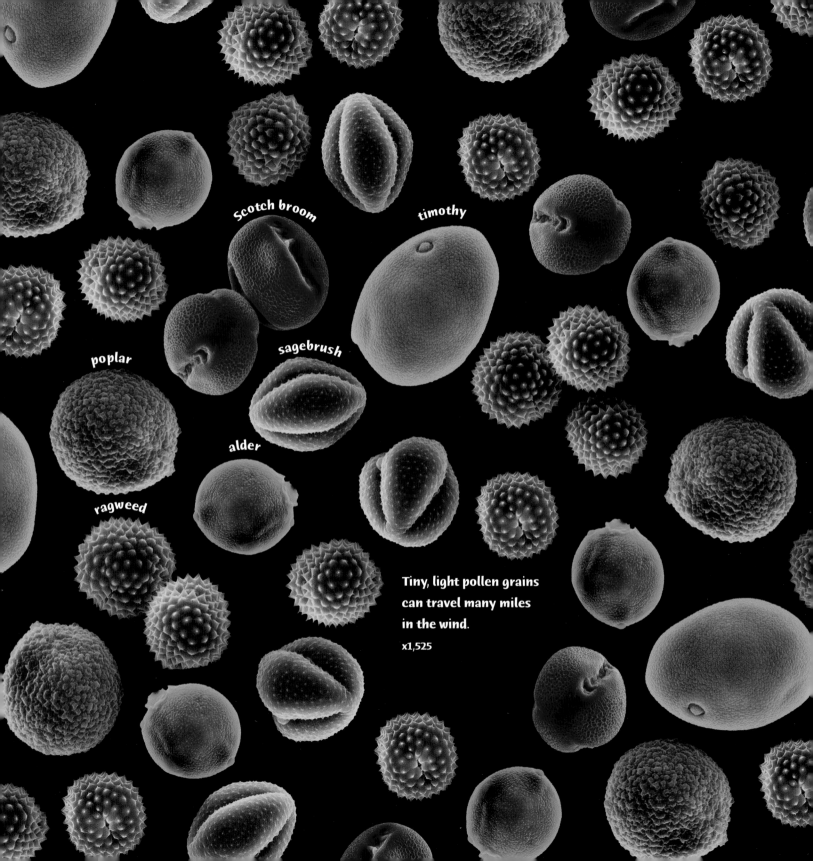

Scotch broom

timothy

poplar

sagebrush

alder

ragweed

Tiny, light pollen grains
can travel many miles
in the wind.

x1,525

"Pass the pepper, please," Isaiah says.

Isaiah's nose twitches as he breathes in the pungent-smelling ground pepper. Pepper, known as the king of spices, contains an irritating chemical called piperine.

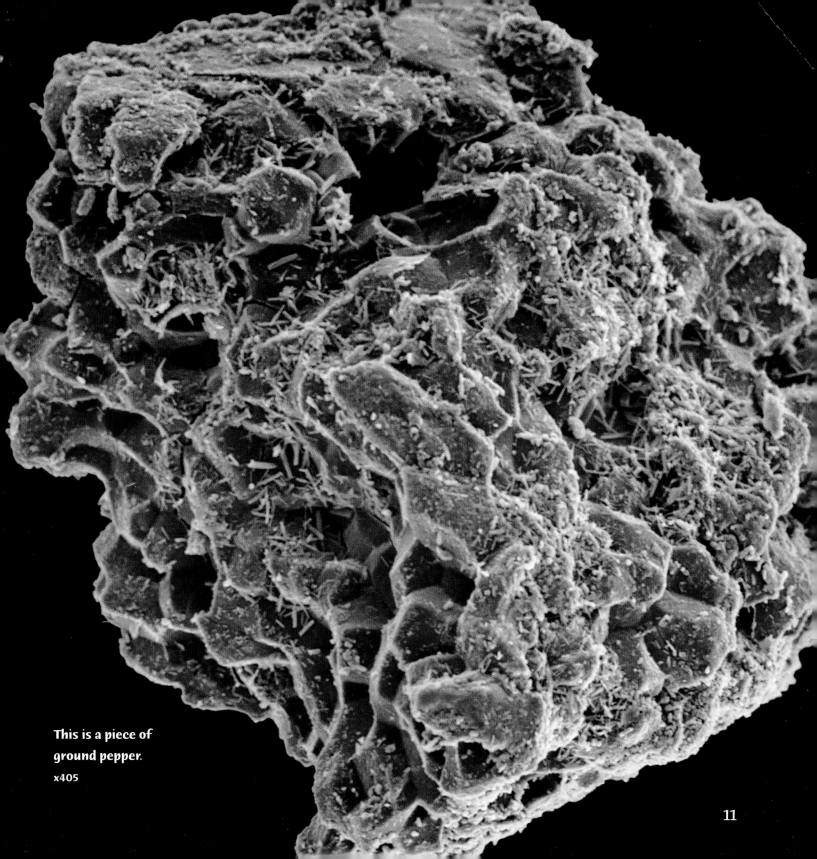

This is a piece of
ground pepper.
x405

11

"Grandma," says Sydney, "come look at this picture."

Although Sydney can't see them, there are thousands of tiny spiderlike creatures living in the chair cushions. These dust mites feed on dead skin from people and pets, producing fecal pellets that trigger allergies and asthma.

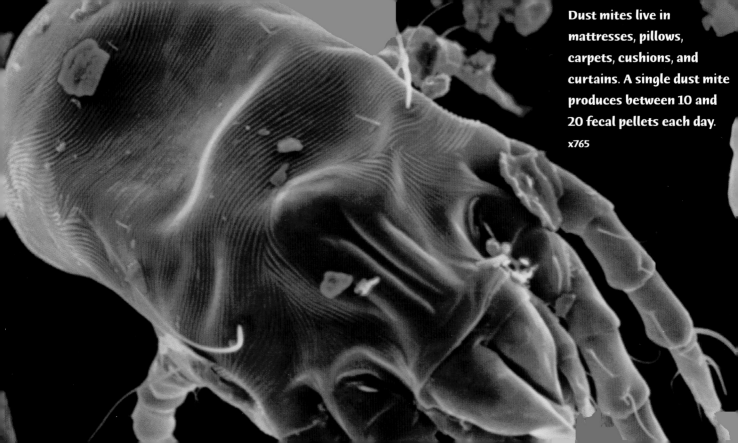

Dust mites live in mattresses, pillows, carpets, cushions, and curtains. A single dust mite produces between 10 and 20 fecal pellets each day.

x765

"Oh, no, the basement sink is leaking," Jonnie mutters.

Jonnie doesn't realize that he's inhaling mold spores made by mildew, a kind of fungus that grows in damp places. A leaky basement faucet is the culprit.

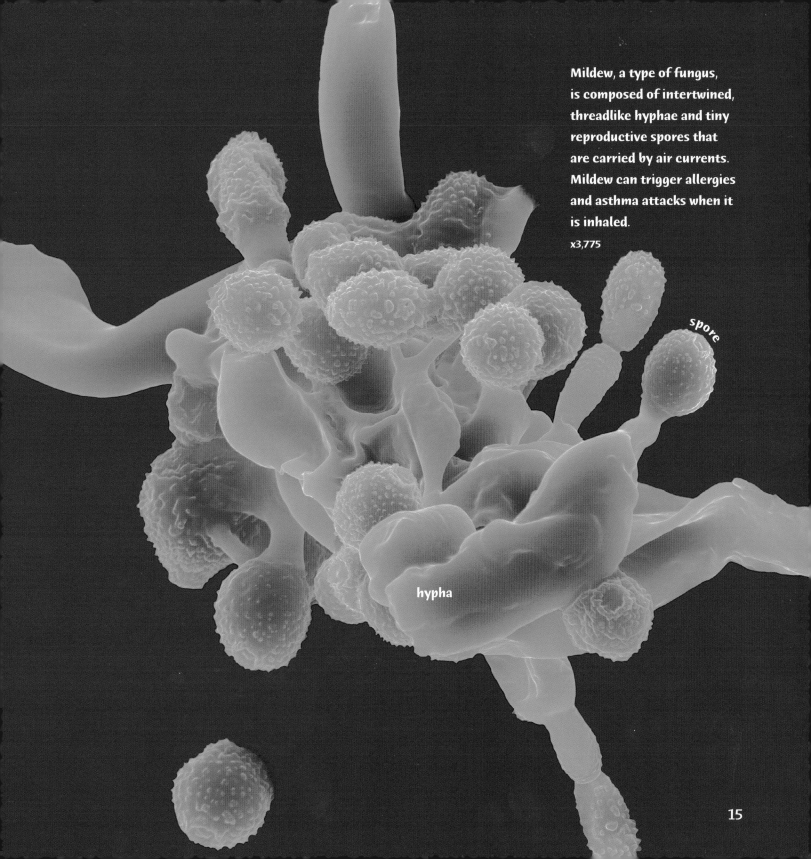

Mildew, a type of fungus,
is composed of intertwined,
threadlike hyphae and tiny
reproductive spores that
are carried by air currents.
Mildew can trigger allergies
and asthma attacks when it
is inhaled.

x3,775

spore

hypha

15

"Why do I have to dust the dresser?" Savionne complains.

Dust is a powerful allergen because it can be composed of several triggers, including pollen, insect waste, and pet dander (the tiny scales from animal hair and skin). Savionne isn't allergic, but her nose is itching anyway. That's because dust is also a physical irritant, made of rough, prickly particles that aggravate the lining of her nose.

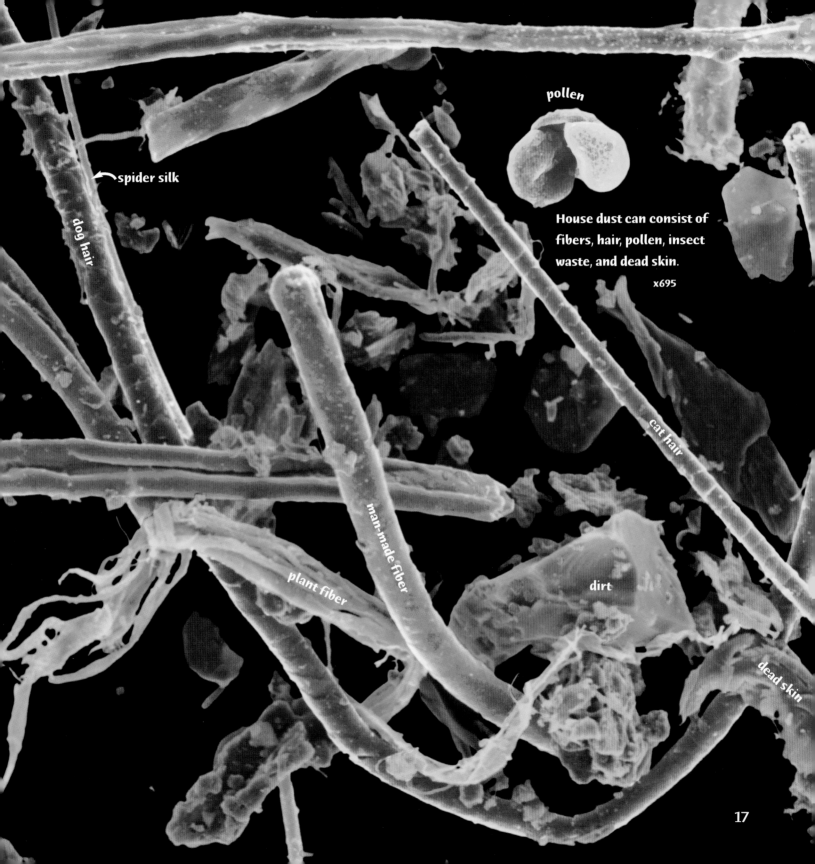

pollen

spider silk

dog hair

House dust can consist of
fibers, hair, pollen, insect
waste, and dead skin.

x695

cat hair

man-made fiber

plant fiber

dirt

dead skin

17

"The pillow popped!" shouts Jeremiah.

The fluff of goose down inside Jeremiah's nose has jagged edges and pointed tips. No wonder his nose is so tickly.

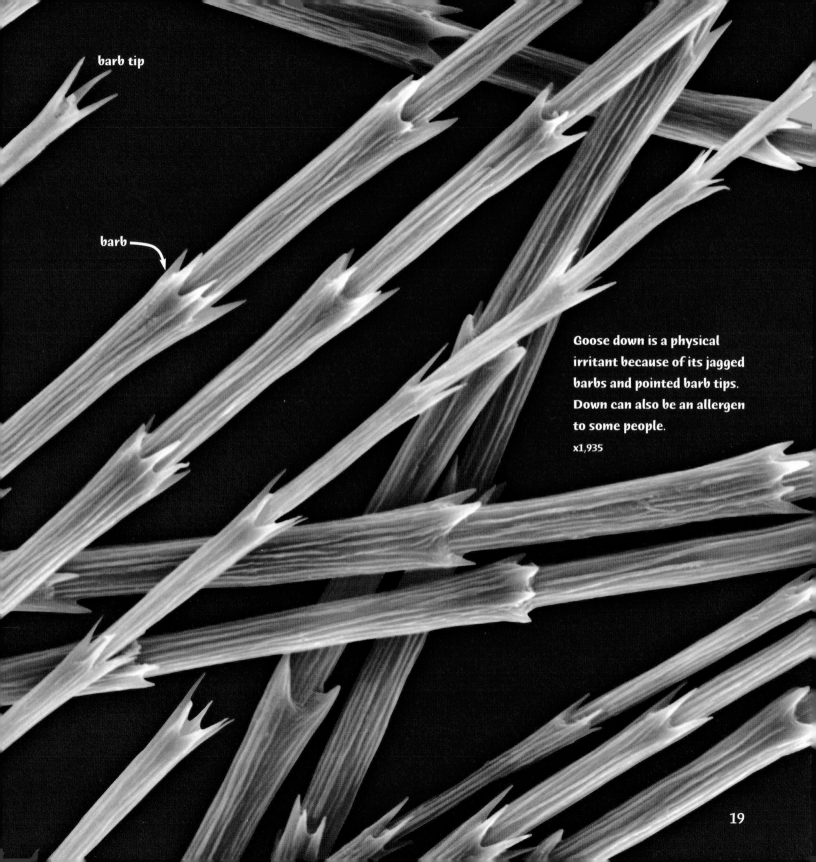

barb tip

barb

Goose down is a physical
irritant because of its jagged
barbs and pointed barb tips.
Down can also be an allergen
to some people.

x1,935

19

"It's not fair!" Montana pouts. "I want to go to the party."

Montana's body is under attack—by a nasty flu virus. Infection-fighting white blood cells rush into her nose where they surround and destroy the virus. Dead cells and virus particles are blown out with the thick mucus that causes uncomfortable nasal congestion. Montana's nose is so stuffy that she's used up a whole box of tissues.

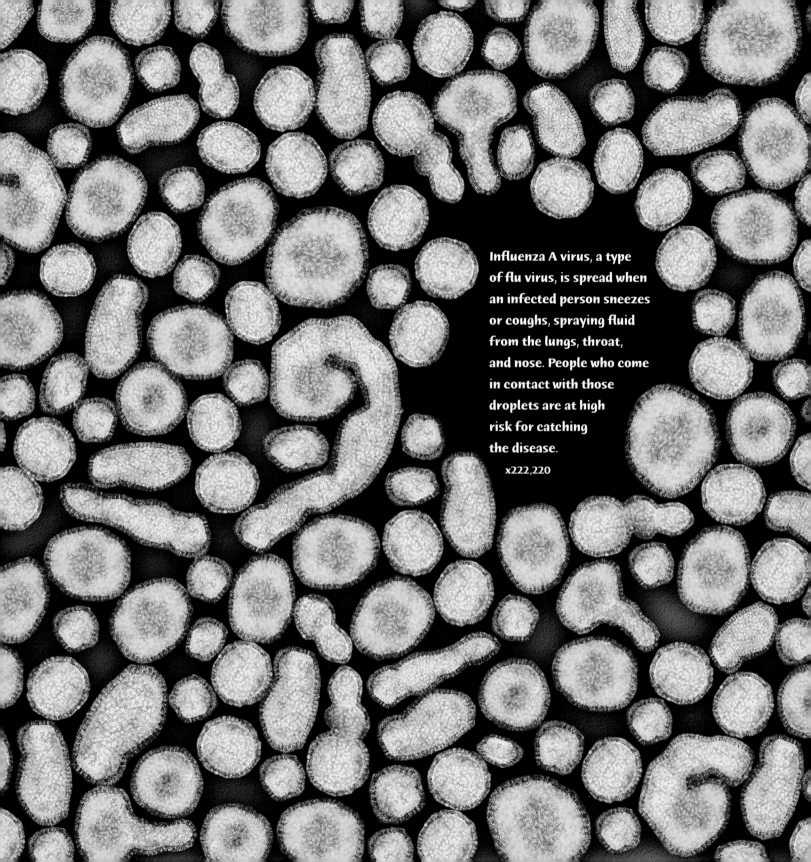

Influenza A virus, a type of flu virus, is spread when an infected person sneezes or coughs, spraying fluid from the lungs, throat, and nose. People who come in contact with those droplets are at high risk for catching the disease.

x222,220

"Here, Kitty!" calls Leo.

Kitty's fur is soft to touch, but inside Leo's nose it feels scratchy and coarse. It's also covered with dander, doubling the danger.

Cat hair (two types shown here) can trigger a sneeze by causing physical irritation, while the dander on the hair is an allergen.

x1,770

dander

dander

"Wait up!" Cody calls.

Sudden bright sunshine is making Cody's nose itch. Mixed-up messages between his eyes and nose are to blame.

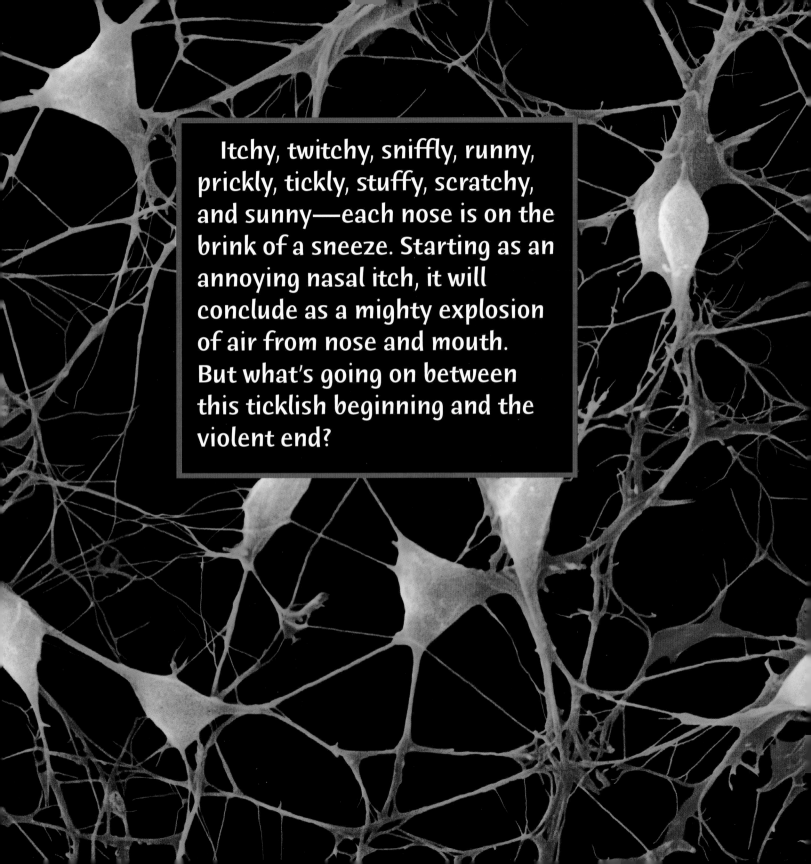

Itchy, twitchy, sniffly, runny, prickly, tickly, stuffy, scratchy, and sunny—each nose is on the brink of a sneeze. Starting as an annoying nasal itch, it will conclude as a mighty explosion of air from nose and mouth. But what's going on between this ticklish beginning and the violent end?

A sneeze is a reflex, an automatic reaction that can't be stopped once it starts. Every sneeze follows the same pathway. It moves quickly, like electricity through wires. But the wires that transmit a sneeze are alive. This tangled network of high-speed transmission lines is made of nerve cells called neurons.

Cells are called the building blocks of life because they are the smallest working parts of living tissues. In the human body there are many kinds of cells—each with a purpose. Red blood cells carry oxygen, white blood cells fight infection, skin cells form a protective covering, and nerve cells—or neurons— transmit messages.

A neuron consists of an axon, a cell body, and dendrites. Neurons are the basic building blocks of the nervous system, which includes the brain and spinal cord. The nervous system is responsible for coordinating all activities of the body. x3,215

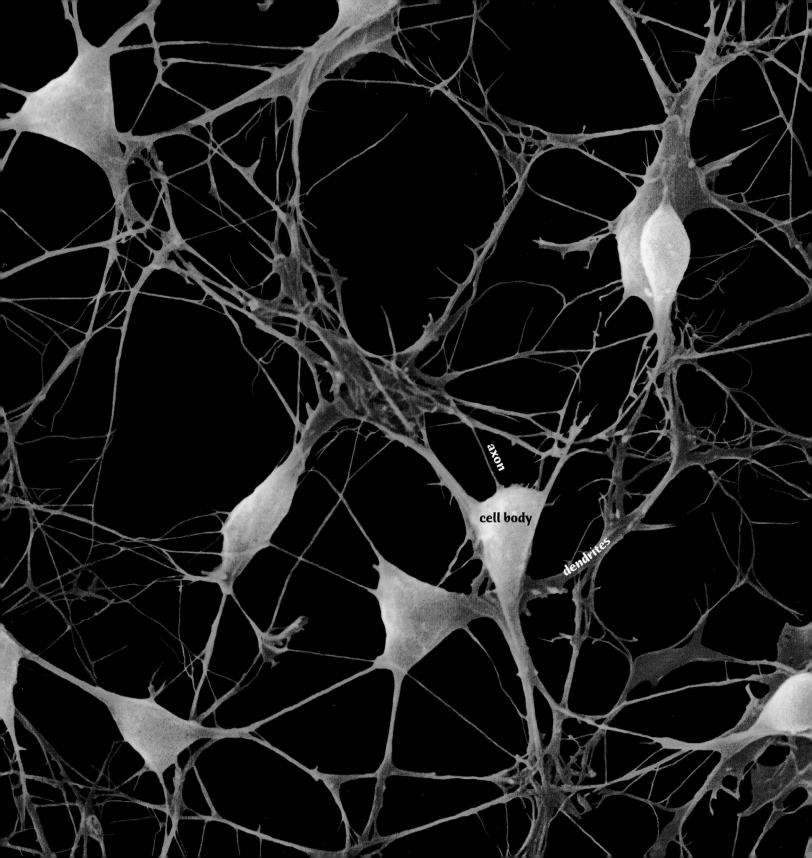

axon

dendrite

As Jeremiah continues the pillow fight, the ticklish feeling inside his nose intensifies as a fluff of down irritates nerve endings. This sensation begins in a neuron, which fires an electrical message, or impulse.

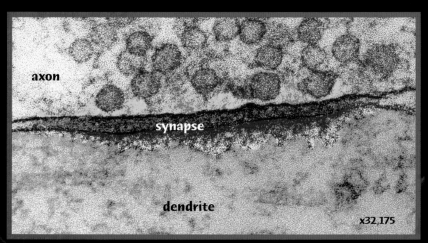

axon

synapse

dendrite

x32,175

This image above shows the synapse (yellow, brown, and purple stripe), or connection point, between an axon (red) of one neuron and the dendrite of another (green). Tiny sacs, called synaptic vesicles (purple circles), in the axon release chemical messengers called neurotransmitters that trigger or inhibit a new impulse in the connecting dendrite.

cell body

x8,795

The electrical impulse zips along the axon until it arrives at the synapse, the point of communication between two neurons. Although the space between the connecting neurons is only 30 nanometers wide—the width of 1/1,000 of a human hair—the impulse cannot jump across. Instead, miniature sacs inside the tip of the axon release chemical messengers into the space. Like a key in a lock, these chemical messengers must match exactly with receptors on the next neuron. The chemical messengers and receptors can either trigger or inhibit a new electrical impulse when the key fits into the lock.

One neuron can fire impulses hundreds of times per second. Because of these repeated firings, messages travel continuously and rapidly throughout the body.

The tickly message originating inside Jeremiah's nose is sent to the sneeze center in the part of his brain stem called the medulla oblongata. The sneeze center responds instantly, like an echo, sending messages back to the nose, which begins to drip. Now Jeremiah's eyes are watering as messages rapidly fire back and forth. In the same instant, the sneeze center fires into Jeremiah's spinal cord.

Now the message is about to

brain

nerve endings

sneeze center

Spinal cord

axon

myelin sheath

This is a cross section of
an axon (green) wrapped
in a myelin sheath (red).
Myelin is a fatty insulating
material that also helps
the impulse travel as fast
as 100 meters per second
(224 miles per hour).

x184,825

Jeremiah hasn't had time to think about the sneeze impulse that has been zooming through his body. But he will feel its effect instantaneously.

The impulse signals neurons that leave Jeremiah's spinal cord. Connected to muscle cells, these neurons release neurotransmitters that make muscles move.

Jeremiah closes his eyes. The muscles in his face and throat tense and tighten, while those in his chest and stomach squeeze . . .

Skeletal muscle is attached to bone or tendons, which are strong bands that connect muscle to bone. When an impulse from a neuron reaches a muscle cell, the muscle contracts or relaxes, depending on the signal. During a sneeze, muscles in the face, chest, throat, and stomach contract in a specific order. These instructions are hardwired in the brain's sneeze center and spinal cord. This means that the sneeze reflex happens exactly the same way every time.
x935

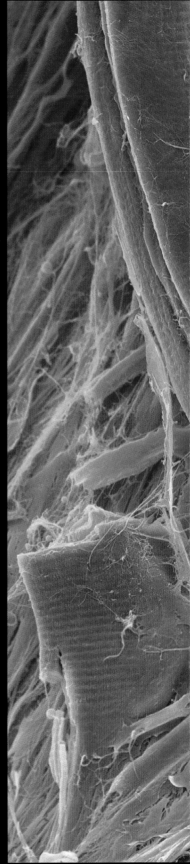

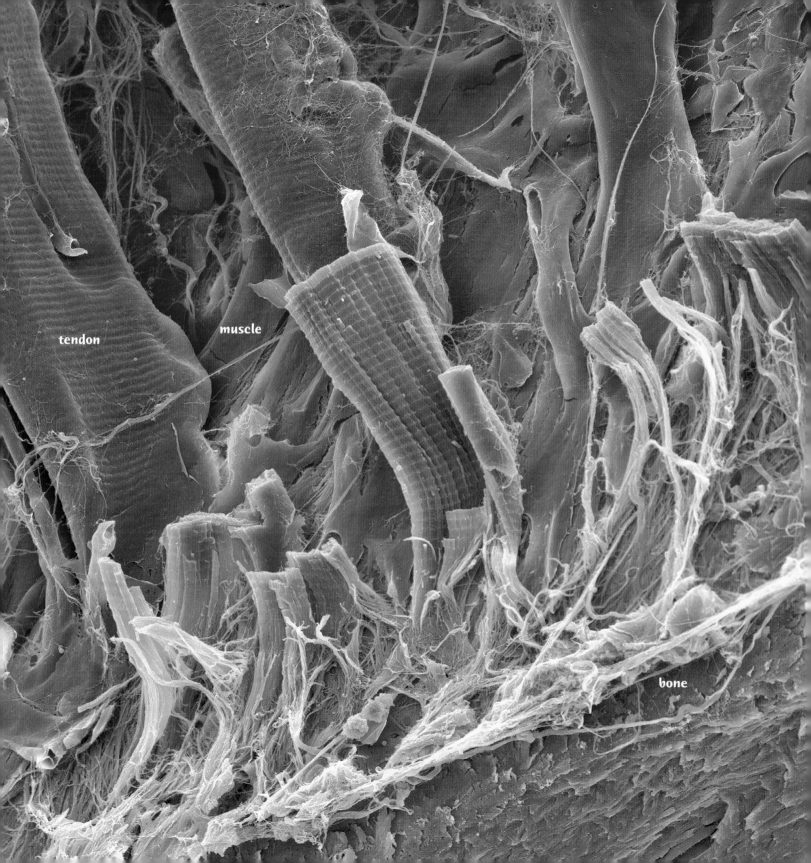

. . . squashing millions of miniature air-filled balloons deep inside his lungs. Air explodes through microscopic airways, and Jeremiah—along with all the other kids—can't hold it back no matter how hard he tries.

Rushing through nine windpipes, warm, moist air bursts from nine noses and mouths at a speed of 100 miles per hour!

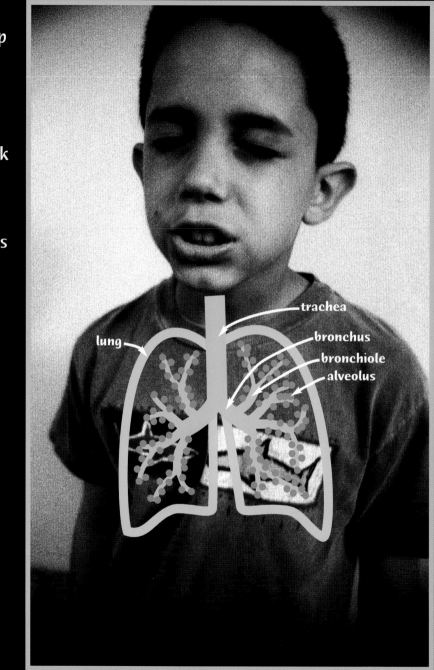

trachea
bronchus
bronchiole
alveolus
lung

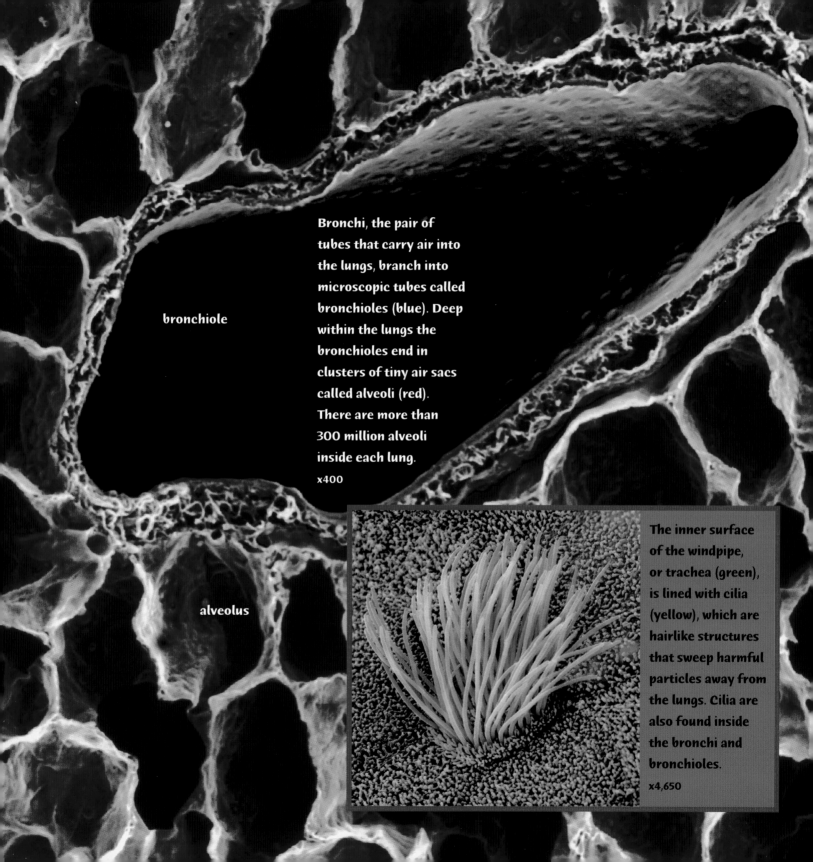

bronchiole

alveolus

Bronchi, the pair of tubes that carry air into the lungs, branch into microscopic tubes called bronchioles (blue). Deep within the lungs the bronchioles end in clusters of tiny air sacs called alveoli (red). There are more than 300 million alveoli inside each lung.
x400

The inner surface of the windpipe, or trachea (green), is lined with cilia (yellow), which are hairlike structures that sweep harmful particles away from the lungs. Cilia are also found inside the bronchi and bronchioles.
x4,650

"ACHOO!"

Nine sneezes for nine reasons: pollen, pepper, mites, mold, dust, down, disease, a hair, and sunshine.

Spraying . . .

spontaneous . . .

sudden . . .

strident . . .

strong . . .

swift . . .

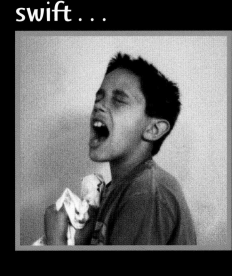

sickly . . .

smelly . . .

surprising . . .

. . . and also splendid. A dance done in an instant by an ensemble of microscopic performers, hardwired never to miss a step.

That's nothing to sneeze at!

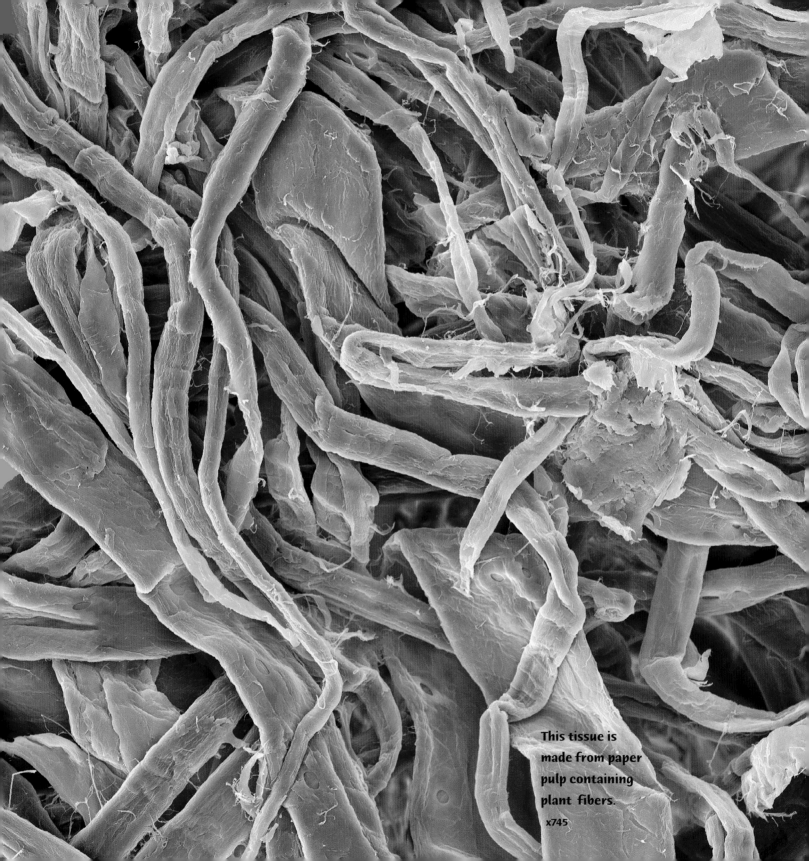

This tissue is made from paper pulp containing plant fibers.

x745

More About Sneezing

The purpose of a sneeze is to dislodge and remove foreign particles from the nose and throat. During a sneeze, air travels at 100 miles per hour, spewing germs from the nose and mouth in a wet spray that can radiate five feet. So please cover your nose and your mouth when you sneeze, and don't forget to wash your hands!

- Over the centuries and throughout the world, sneezing has been associated with superstition. Nursery rhymes instructed how sneezes brought both good luck and bad, and many cultures thought that sneezing forced evil spirits out of the body.
- The custom of saying "God bless you" after a person sneezes originated in Rome during the papacy of Pope Gregory VII (AD 540–604). The bubonic plague, a gruesome disease that caused black swellings on its victims as well as making them cough and sneeze, was raging through Europe, killing millions. The pope suggested saying "May God bless you" after a person sneezed, in hopes that the prayer would protect the person from the plague and certain death.
- Babies, young children, and animals sneeze through their noses, while adults usually sneeze through their mouths.
- People don't sneeze when asleep because some of the nerves involved in the sneeze reflex are also resting.
- It's estimated that between 18 and 35 percent of the population sneezes when exposed to sudden bright light. Called ACHOO syndrome (for "autosomal dominant compelling helioophthalmic outburst"), it is an inherited condition that happens when a message received by the optic nerve from the eyes causes nasal itching by triggering impulses in nerves in the nose.
- Some people sneeze while plucking their eyebrows. This occurs when nerve endings in the face are irritated and fire an impulse that reaches a nasal nerve.
- Pinching the nose on the brink of a sneeze can occasionally relieve nasal irritation enough to stop a sneeze reflex.

The first-ever copyrighted motion picture was of a sneeze. In 1888, Thomas Edison started experimenting with motion pictures. He'd already invented the phonograph, which played recorded sounds, and announced: "I am experimenting upon an instrument which does for the eye what the phonograph does for the ear." He reasoned that if he made a record of motion as it is seen with the eyes, then it could be played back in real time.

Over the next five years, Edison and his assistants worked on the idea—perfecting the Kinetograph, a machine to record moving images; and the Kinetoscope, a machine used to view a motion picture. They finally recorded *The Edison Kinetoscopic Record of a Sneeze*. The movie starred Fred Ott, an Edison employee who was photographed while pretending to sneeze.

The Library of Congress copyrighted the motion picture on January 9, 1894.

About the Micrographs

The color photographs in *Sneeze!* are called electron micrographs because they were taken with either a scanning electron microscope (SEM) or a transmission electron microscope (TEM). The SEM views a subject's surface and can magnify it 10 to 500,000 times. The TEM views a subject's interior features and requires that samples are prepared as extremely thin slices. The TEM magnifies an object 500 to 1 million times.

Unlike light microscopes, which have glass lenses and use visible white light to magnify a subject, electron microscopes have electromagnetic lenses (circular magnets) and use electrons to magnify. Electrons are invisible, high-energy subatomic particles. Compared to visible light wavelengths, electrons have a shorter wavelength and produce greater detail and higher magnification.

Because electrons are not within the visible light spectrum, SEM and TEM micrographs are first produced as black-and-white images. It is impossible to know the true colors of highly magnified structures, so colors are chosen and added to the images in a computer program, making it possible to highlight interesting features, emphasize contrasting areas, or simply create a beautiful image. Shown below is the original black-and-white SEM micrograph of a cluster of neurons. Two different colored versions of the same original image highlight structures.

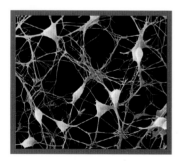 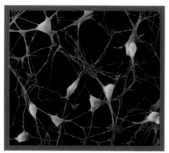 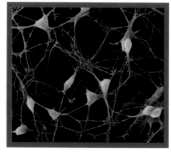

Resources

American Treasures of the Library of Congress: A Sneeze Caught on Film
http://www.loc.gov/exhibits/treasures/trr018.html
Learn more about Thomas Edison's historic motion picture of a sneeze.

Asthma and Allergy Foundation of America
http://www.aafa.org/
Learn more about asthma and allergies and find support groups for asthma sufferers.

Dennis Kunkel's Educational Website
http://education.denniskunkel.com/
Browse the image library, use the interactive features, and find additional information about microscopy.

Kramer, Stephen, and Dennis Kunkel. *Hidden Worlds: Looking Through a Scientist's Microscope*. Boston: Houghton Mifflin Company, 2001.

Neuroscience for Kids
http://faculty.washington.edu/chudler/neurok.html
This website by Dr. Eric H. Chudler, PhD explains more about the nervous system.

Siy, Alexandra, and Dennis Kunkel. *Mosquito Bite*. Watertown, MA: Charlesbridge Publishing, 2005.

Society for Neuroscience
http://www.sfn.org/
The Society for Neuroscience is the world's largest organization of scientists and physicians dedicated to understanding the nervous system. Go to Publications and click on Brain Facts to download copies of the book *Brain Facts: A Primer on the Brain and Nervous System*.

Glossary

allergen Any substance that causes an allergic reaction. Pollen, dust, pet dander, and mold spores can be allergens (see pages 16, 19, 23).

allergy An unusually high sensitivity to certain substances (such as foods, drugs, microscopic organisms, or irritants) or conditions (such as temperature extremes) that causes the body's immune system to react by releasing histamine. Common allergy symptoms include sneezing, itching, and skin rash (see pages 8, 12, 16, 43).

alveolus (plural: alveoli) A tiny air sac inside the lungs where the exchange of oxygen and carbon dioxide takes place (see pages 34, 35).

asthma A common lung disease marked by a persistent inflammation of the airways. Affected people have episodes when cold air, exercise, or an allergen causes the small airways (bronchioles) inside the lungs to constrict, making breathing difficult (see pages 12, 15, 43).

axon A thin, fiberlike extension of a neuron that carries messages to other neurons or muscle cells (see pages 26, 27, 28, 29, 31).

barb A tiny branch growing out of the shaft of a feather (see page 19).

brain stem The part of the human brain where the spinal cord connects to the cerebrum. The cerebrum is the upper section of the brain. The brain stem controls involuntary functions of the body such as breathing, heart rate, and blood pressure (see page 30).

bronchiole A tiny, thin-walled tube branching from a bronchus. Alveoli protrude from the respiratory bronchioles (see pages 34, 35).

bronchus (plural: bronchi) One of the two main branches of the windpipe, or trachea, that enters the lungs. At the lungs, bronchi branch into smaller airways called bronchioles (see pages 34, 35).

cell The basic unit of living matter. Cells can function alone or with other cells to perform basic life functions (see pages 20, 26, 28, 32).

cell body The part of a neuron that contains the nucleus, or control center, of the cell (see pages 26, 27, 28, 29).

cilium (plural: cilia) A tiny, hairlike structure found on the surface of some cells. Cilia inside the trachea, bronchi, and bronchioles filter air by sweeping foreign particles away from the lungs (see page 35).

dander Scales and flakes from hair, feathers, or skin (see pages 16, 22, 23).

dendrite A treelike branch of a neuron that receives messages from other neurons (see pages 26, 27, 28, 29).

dust mite A tiny arachnid found in bedding, carpets, and curtains. Mites feed on dead skin from humans and animals (see pages 12, 13, 36).

fungus (plural: fungi) A spore-producing organism that thrives in damp environments. Fungi get their food from rotting organic matter (see pages 14, 15).

histamine A chemical released by immune system cells in response to allergens (see page 8).

hypha (**plural: hyphae**) One of the many threadlike structures that form the body of a fungus (see page 15).

immune system The structures and functions of the body that protect it from disease (see page 8).

impulse An electrical signal transmitted along a nerve (see pages 28, 29, 30, 31, 32, 40).

medulla oblongata The part of the brain stem that carries out most involuntary functions such as coughing, breathing, and vomiting (see page 30).

mold A fuzzy growth of tiny fungi that lives on organic matter such as rotting food, cloth, and leather, especially in warm, damp environments (see pages 14, 36).

myelin sheath The compact fatty insulation that surrounds an axon (see page 31).

nanometer A very small unit of measurement (one billionth of a meter) (see page 29).

nervous system The network of nerves within the body, including the brain and spinal cord, that receives sensory information and controls the body's responses (see pages 26, 43).

neuron A cell specialized for generating and transmitting messages. A neuron is composed of a cell body, axon, and dendrites. It is also called a nerve cell (see pages 26, 28, 29, 30, 32).

neurotransmitter A chemical messenger that is released by a neuron at a synapse in order to transfer information to other neurons (see pages 29, 32).

piperine A chemical found in pepper plants (see page 10).

pollen Spores (reproductive cells) produced by a flowering seed plant (see pages 8, 9, 13, 16, 17, 36).

pungent Having a strong smell or taste (see page 10).

reflex An involuntary, or automatic, response (see pages 26, 32, 40).

spinal cord Nervous tissue found inside the backbone. The spinal cord carries impulses to and from the brain (see pages 26, 30, 32).

spontaneous Involuntary or instinctive movement (see page 36).

spore A reproductive cell produced by plants, fungi, and some microorganisms (see pages 14, 15).

strident Loud (see page 37).

synapse The point of connection where messages are transferred from the axon of one neuron to the dendrites of another (see page 29).

synaptic vesicle A tiny bubblelike sac that releases neurotransmitters into the synapse (see page 29).

tendon Bands of tissue that attach muscle to bone (see pages 32, 33).

trachea The tube, or windpipe, that carries air into and out of the body (see pages 34, 35).

virus A microorganism that uses a living cell to reproduce and causes disease in its host (see pages 20, 21).

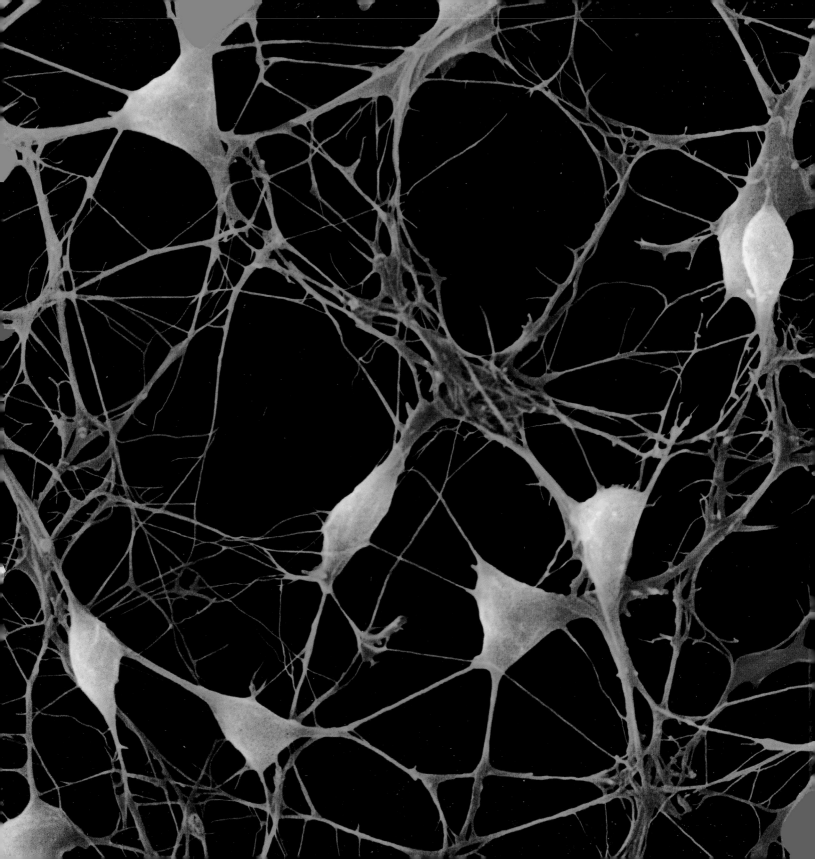